More praise for *Lepr*

"Lise Goett's *Leprosarium* is luminous, symphonic, and suffused with mystical awareness—a primer on learning to live with despair and silence, to be *tempered by suffering* and also calm, inflamed by desire and yet arrive at acceptance of silence itself as God. In her intricately constructed asylum for incurables we come upon a host of artists and saints, lovers, *a warden of extinguished hopes, / keeper of the stillnesses, avatar / of what is past.* The allusive range is breathtaking, the diction precisely chiseled. It is as if we have taken the hand of a contemporary Virgil on a journey from the ancient world to our own stopping off to look at images mounted in a gallery of hard-won realizations. Certain lines will stay with me forever: *The body is a prison with a key.* When we enter *Leprosarium* we enter at once a work of brilliant lyric art and ecstatic vision."
—Carolyn Forché

"These bold poems . . . so exquisitely wrought, find their subject in art, history, religion, and day-to-day life, focusing on the tense line between vulnerability and power. . . . This is dangerous art, as serious as a heart attack, unsparing mostly of the poet herself, and as intensely rewarding as it is unsettling. . . . The clear intelligence and imagination of these poems make them as much homage to what they question as they are an act of resistance."
—from Toi Derricotte's judge's citation for the Robert
H. Winner Memorial Award of the Poetry Society of America

"In *Leprosarium* (asylum for lepers) Lise Goett 'explains,' quoting two lines from *King Lear:* 'The art of our necessities is strange, / That can make vile things precious.' In the final poem of this magnificent set of poems, Goett gives us the agonizing impossibility of a young nurse's life in the sole American leprosarium, in the town of Carville, Louisiana: 'Come for the sycamores and oaks, the manacled light. // You'd have to be half crazy / or in love to do the work. Then learn to sit // with your despair and bear / the silence of God that is.' [A] various but amazingly sustained book."
—Richard Howard

"With elegance of mind and music, now sinuous as woodwinds, now forceful as an unexpected chord progression, Goett's poetic lines are able to suggest states of glory and splendor before vanishing again into the hard kernel of

verbal custody—into 'glister' and 'slurry'—into formal and acoustic fulfillment. Feminine eroticism under the aegis of patriarchy inform several meditations on the art of Leonardo, Fragonard, Rodin, Singer Sargent, Whistler, and Leonor Fini. With self-possession and discernment, Goett has crafted a book of intellectual drive and irrefutable grace in poems that wrestle with humanity's stewardship or annihilation of all that is wild and passionate at the core of existence."
—Roberto Tejada

"With her masterly soundscapes, multi-colored symphonies, and ekphrastic meditations, it's clear Lise Goett is an impassioned chatelaine of sound ('Eros Aprilling us into wider spaces') and visual beauty, but most of all, she revels in the *frissons*, the firefly sparks that virtuosic language can liberate. With a saint's or a dervish's acuity, she insists, of this 'spinning lazaretto' of a world: 'Everything is grist for ascendance.' Indeed, in her cascading lines, rife with probity and complexity, soaring and suffering appear as close as Damon and Pythias. Drawn to defiance and disavowal as much as to ecstasy and devotion, Goett declares, in the brilliant, betrayed persona of Camille Claudel, the tragic sculptor: 'I am wild like the nettle and dangerous / behind the gate.' What a consistently astute, lush, and startling collection!"
—Cyrus Cassells

"Goett continuously seeks to name despair in order to move toward a more intimate relationship with the self and the world. 'Every era has its St. Prassede wringing her bloody sponge. . . .' Goett knows how to make her readers squirm, and when she's at her linguistically contorted best she offers complex understandings of the ways pain, disillusionment, and hope intersect."
—*Publishers Weekly*

LEPROSARIUM

LISE GOETT

Tupelo Press
North Adams, Massachusetts

Library of Congress Cataloging-in-Publication Data available upon request.
ISBN: 978-1-946482-03-7

Cover and text designed and composed in Horley Oldstyle by Bill Kuch.

Cover and title page art: John Singer Sargent (American, 1856–1925),
Fumée d'ambre gris (Smoke of Ambergris), 1880. Oil on canvas, $54\,{}^{3}\!/_{4}$ x $35\,{}^{11}\!/_{16}$
inches (139.1 x 90.6 cm). Sterling and Francine Clark Art Institute,
Williamstown, Massachusetts, 1955.15. Image copyright © Sterling and
Francine Clark Art Institute, Williamstown, Massachusetts, USA (photo by
Michael Agee).

First edition: February 2018.

Tupelo Press
P.O. Box 1767, North Adams, Massachusetts 01247
(413) 664–9611 / editor@tupelopress.org / www.tupelopress.org

Tupelo Press is an award-winning independent literary press that publishes
fine fiction, nonfiction, and poetry in books that are a joy to hold as well as read.
Tupelo Press is a registered 501(c)(3) nonprofit organization, and we rely on
public support to carry out our mission of publishing extraordinary work
that may be outside the realm of the large commercial publishers. Financial
donations are welcome and are tax deductible.

—for Richard Howard

Contents

Leprosarium

The art of our necessities is strange,
That can make vile things precious.

—*King Lear*, III, ii

Symphony in White, No. 1: The White Girl

—after Whistler

But for this,
the power of the girl's virginity—

her chasuble with its intimations of untainted
white—there is no angel of annunciation.

A single stem of loosestrife dangles from her distaff hand,
the bouquet's other flowers having fallen to the floor.

She stands upon the body of a bear, seeming
to float above it,

never touching what decomposes, her slipper
striking its head like the foot of the Mother of God.

No intimation of the closeness of a Master's breath,
yet the accouterments of Presence are felt, if not

depicted, a universe at hand as yet unseen, the fulcrum
of some event about to tip in her direction:

her demeanor a village calm before a devastation,
before the riders arrive with their polished mounts and handsome guns.

And so that some history of the Master's empire may be played out in her,
she says, *Let it be done to me,*

pinioned as she is in this bridled order
as amber mortifies the fly,

so that when we compare the vibrant, sherry-colored,
glass-bead eyes of the beast

to hers, we begin to apprehend a symphony in white
(as transformative as the torrent of a blizzard

and as coldly alluring
and all that it has muted and all that it has drowned out)

and wonder, between the girl and the bear,
which the corpse and which the trophy.

Epoch

—*after A. R. Ammons*

When you consider the bee, that it does not exhaust its generosity, betraying
the vanity of the giver, but pours its radiance into every
gallery of the comb; when you consider the host hunger

of the keeper who cannot make his own sweetness but
sings his greed into every cell with his smoker and veil,
heed the unspoken, heed his incarnadine need, heed the tintinnabulation

of his gold censor against its ecclesial chain.
Beneath a surface coiffed to diadem lies a leprosarium.
Bonneted in scrim, the keeper narcotizes the bee.

When you consider the silence in which each being gives itself up
to the ravener, lover to loved, ingot of amber to be extracted,
bow to the thing most vulnerable, splayed in innocence, open to be wounded,

waxwing or woad, vixen or vole, lichen or leach,
each the beggar of its own circumstance.
Wastrel, wound less in chill when the colony is cold,

the netherworld of your appetite tolling.
The unexalted thing that gives most utterly, wantonly, gives once to exhaustion.
In the muscled dark, the sweetmeat unhinges.

High above, in an attic of leaves,
the gray husk of the world waits to be emptied
until nothing reaps save wind on the barrens—

hollowed, unhallowed, abandoned, the world
a papery casket. Epoch, when will you listen?
They are the oracles of this, the bees.

The Cutters

Summer spindles us, the cutters:
azure for eternity, sapphire for memory,

cobalt for oblivion. Down the delphinium walk,
blue-veined and lipped, we ply the tourniquet,

limn ourselves with crosses. What makes us cut?
Who calls us from the dead, sable-throated?

Who convenes us, blade to flesh, pain hauled
writhing from the depths, unelemented?

Radiant, crosshatched where we hone
a purgatory of days of distance from the source—

not the furied blood of beasts hurried
to the stanchion, but willed, wild thralling.

Self-inflicted, this is fire work! We cutters gall
ourselves as fire wounds the wood.

Sibylline, we glide in our scarab-covered coracles,
waiting for an oracle.

Unheavened, hounded, self-abandoned,
witness the spectacle of our page ant:

blood-garneted, garreted with the five-wound spar,
saints who suffer voices into something rich and strange,

chimeras speaking through us.
Augur, mortify us differently. Appease

the knife, our silken mistress. Before the dragnets trawl
for one more martyr, stanch the ceaseless drip

of bitters in the cells, these tups and wethers of neurosis.
Curried, blindered, self-afflicted,

pain out to no one save ourselves,
century, witness us, the martyrs.

Symphony in Red

—for an Aries

And in July, when the harlot weathers mount
their temperatures, we, conceived during the dog-star hours,

wear the mark of who we are, our origins
bearing down upon the bodies of our parents, their sloe-ginned

rut. And in January, when others are asleep
or think us so, we are coupling, snow leopards in heat.

Come into our abode, and we will make you glow
like blonde sun on hoary snow.

As members of that other scarlet college whose emoluments
reside in lubricious tongues, who bump and grind as if a parliament

of engines were invested in our loins,
and pray divine offices on skin, our coin

of realm—carnal, labial, red cardinals of the universal
church of mouths and tongues that resemble

the swags of bunting you were wrapped in—
we glory in the red of man as meat becoming

animal. Give us your tongue and we will suck
you in. We will lick you into luck. We will suck and suckle

you—largo, then quick. You,
our prey, we pray to bed you.

We are more full of flame
and voices than shades that abide the dark. Have no shame.

Passion is the Passion.
If flesh be beaten into light, pass

through us as if we were fire,
flame, the narrow gate: by this you are

measured. Do you think God dead?
Give us your head, and we will show you heaven.

We who are conceived in summer heat, as is our nature,
burn.

Dementia Rag

Do we have to travel tonight? Do we have to travel?
I've already crisscrossed the continent three times tonight
without recourse to plane or broom.

But haven't we shiny little potties!
All clatter and shine, neglect looks very clean.
(I can tell by the plumbing that we're no longer in America.)

Let's say, for argument's sake,
that we're on the Mediterranean
in a villa with a balustrade that brocades the light of our decline.

The attendants, how they love to patronize!
They're always asking me what day it is,
Saturday or Wednesday.

Does it matter what day or month it is?
Does it matter whether May or June?
When you're dying, it's always the hallowed time of year.

My daughters are my sisters now.
Does it really matter who they are
if I've checked all the lists but failed to say:

there are more important kinds of failure
than those of heart or spleen?
My, how we old love gathering our wools.

Do we have to travel tonight?
At least we'll be going by horse, not car.
Hitch up the fat-wheeled wagon then.

Does it really matter? Does it matter yet?
Death assails the question
of when I'll be going. Soon.

The Passion

—*for Matthew Shepard*

In April, the gullies fill with the bodies of boys
ready to be broken like milkweed,
ravened by winter,

its Lent of no hosannas,
the sanctuary already darkened and draped for the Passion—
these boys who close their eyes

to live in heat,
to stay sepulchered there,
treading to the heart's mnemonic,

massaging their solitudes
until gilt into the glistening dough
that will be braided and broken.

In April, a raw flowering moves northward
in the coifs of the trees;
and these boys open, shafts

umbelled and sheathed,
like improbable flowers named for the Passion,
trumpeting their blood,

in search of the lost grove
where Christ gave up his secret,
his turbulent, disturbed divinity,

as they cry:
We are the good thieves who stole Paradise,
flushed from the brake as quarry.

At dusk, we appear,
asking asylum,
drawn to your farmhouse grate,

your bed shackled in light,
and peer at those invisible couplings
that bind the pure to their captors

who confound our ecstasy with punishment
until carrion come,
the tomb plundered.

Symphony in Black: *Madame X*

The stark expanse and pallor of her skin
spell the largesse of seduction. Her hipbones jut

slightly forward, her haunch—the leg and loin
considered together as in: *a haunch of deer*—a citadel.

Beneath her gown the outline of a frigate,
the fallen strap of her gown's jet hourglass

the entryway to a private vestibule of fantasy,
her bodice on the precipice of meeting the salon's parquet

where surrender is no longer in question,
but what will be paid for this unveiling

of her power in full panoply,
this public iteration of want undoing

the spectator
who devours the rhythm of heavy breathing,

her raw, pinkened palm intimating *frisson.*
The portrait is no longer about the poser

(for the poser herself will grow tired of the pose,
listing like a Doric column seated on unstable ground)

but the iris of mind, its speculation:
the brilliantine, hard coupling imagined

in midday, drowning out the daily martyrdom of the poor.
An addict stroking the barrel of a syringe,

the spectator becomes the portrait
of an artist entrapped in his own snare:

the anticipation, the knowing
of the clearly erotic chute of black:

the graying out, the going under
that one prays for as one falls.

Flame-Shirt Rag

Love, you come lit with a fifth of alcohol,
always asking from your Cross to be taken down.
Your shirt split open, your heart wrapped in barbs,
Robe of Nessus, Sacred Heart, how can I put you on

without being burned? In the spectral hours, you visit me
in my fine, stone house, ask for a piece of bread,
show me your wounded heart and where the nails and shiv went in.
Immolated in their seamless shirts of flame,

the young are up to no good again, shrouded in an ether dream.
I stay awake, as mothers do, worrying about the outcome.
I have had to cut my heart out to try to get some sleep.
You look down from your Cross and say,

What can you do to me that you haven't already done?
Tell me a story of resurrection and of a better life.
Tell me that I'll get home to heaven after all.
I've had my nervous breakdown. I've had electric shock.

I've had my figurative lobotomy, courtesy of patriarchy
and the cops. Your ladies of heaven look on the contraband of war
I'm always smuggling out. I'm running out of time.
O Sacred Victim, send me the clippings from your fingernails.

I need to resist temptation—another high in care
of Robitussin, airplane glue, naphtha,
the mechanical phallus, a whiff from an aluminum tube.
O fig tree planted in a prison yard, Liberty tattooed with a Molotov,

I can't die trying to love you enough.
Further, farther, faster, this life,
the passing scenery, and tarmac a blur,
o moonbeam on a sugar plate,

all I want is ecstasy and a lover who makes me wet.
In the carceral imagination, all of us are trapped.
Sometimes the mind and body are out of phase,
the dim boy in me the only one who claps.

Molest the Dead

I.

Molest the dead. Pluck from them their buried
honey. Envy them their past perfect
tense, their had done and hurried gone. Harry
them, for bars of iron cannot deter

their passing. Hate, heat, hoar cannot injure
their integument nor corrupt what worms
have gowned and mastered with their ferried van lines
of dispersal. Goader, flenser of squirming

flesh, we, the warm, the unstill living, speak
dog, bark the invisible as it shakes
the foundations of the house. Bush, speak.
Must I begin the conversation? I quake,

I listen, I brake fast, I bell the stray
to warn the lark away, then seize the day.

II.

You, called rubbish in the public fracas
of the world, I would choir you with the thees
and thous of Quakers, rub gasoline, strike match,
for you are flame come to raze the world. Beneath

your heat, I am roiling in a cauldron.
I betray you, and you send me doves.
Your Panza, I am confused. Send squall,
eternal cold, for I am storm and love

the lightning. Señor, you need more phlegmatic
friends. Three collops of hag venison
have put bitters in my stew. Meet me at
the well, or surely I will be in prison

when you get back. I await your reply,
a sign, the merest gesture to decry.

III.

There is no truth in news, no news in truth.
Skoal, my liege. If I am drunk, you are
the bar, the peaches of San Gersolè couth
and sweet. I down these hours, bare

of cartilage, patient some widening
of your breadth within me. Meddler, medlar,
I am that fruit that must rot to ripen,
rind browning on the branch until made

ready for your pluck, your coming. I stand
impeached. I love the flesh, its flush, its foison
under eager hands, the skin's glissando—
and sex, how its truth lights up the dark, moistens

the arid desert in us, heaven
leavened or made hollow—by your leave.

IV.

In the witching hours of dissolution,
there are some who travel on dark ice,
fetching, by their troth, delusion
to ferry them to safety. Wheel of Vice,

Lady Luck is their fortune, whirling in their
want. Their fervors adamant and obvious
with their single-pointed want to harrow
and be harrowed, they are flagrant in their must.

Who am I to judge them, brazen Jezebel
or belle of Jesus? (Up or down the funicular,
Venus is never done.) Levy your gabelle
on my tiny mind of salt. But when the wick

of night is spent, the bull cannot be trusted,
and the hotwife grows hotter for her lust.

V.

There where the meadow has been razed
by fire, I have been razed. I beg you. I have
as yet no feeling: my life a little maze
of works, of Bedlamite behaviors

gone up in flame. My argument with you?
I am living and wish to stay so. Then take
me as I am. Love all of me, you
who have drained my cupboards of their reds: steak,

wine, blood, and bid me cut off my hand,
for I am thief and he who draws the knife
gets Isaac. Good enemy, molest what's dead
inside me. Wrack, rend, mold me to new life,

but chide me gently, for I, the blasted,
abjure the blast, the silence after.

VI.

Every being wants ecstasy, that moment
when, no longer fearful of its own
divinity, the angel of the body
approaches, the tomb opened, the stone

loosed at last. Star-root, who are you?
I who have made a cottage industry
of adoring you in that beautiful young
man on the cross seek you now in leaf

light, in deer scat, in the interstices
of things, where, in the coincidence
of opposites, you reside, waiting to seize
our attention, out of all its indifferences.

Cadence I will call you for you are always
changing—I, unbending prodigal.

VII.

I choir the Alexandria you are
leaving: your light as principle, the heart
as extra, our compass gimbaled in the dark.
If Armageddon is your way of parting,

I will miss the tintinnabulation
of your spurs. Indeed, I will miss myself
for aren't you the deity who shuns
the lie of who I am, delves deeper, salves

the wounds I inflict? For aren't you *us*?
Aren't we each other? How we fondle
the grenade. We heart you, our scapegoat. Jesus,
humble us for we cannot but offend

the vision we have failed or bring
ourselves to bear our final perishing.

Symphony in Brimstone: *Barn Owl* (Plate 171)

—after Audubon

An owl with the chiseled face of Saturn,
a rodent dangling from his claw:

beneath him, the open maw
of a second ravener,

its posture reminiscent of the ghastly
multitudes of Satan's underlings, flung belly

up, in Bruegel's *The Fall of the Rebel
Angels,* the intensity of the old revolt

to be mirrored once again (and only)
by the terror of the End;

behind the pair:
some prefigurement of the ashen,

snow-cast fields of Armageddon,
when the foundation of everything you thought fixed

and firm, the gods of your idolatry, will be shaken out:
the gun-cotton–colored floes, the Stygian effluence

of plunder, whelms of the lost Carrier of the Light—
you, no longer a spectator of other people's woes

but woebegone tatterdemalion
dangling from the minion's claw.

In the throes of this purgation,
the heart-shaped face will appear

of some angel of Death or Rapture—
you, an underpinning tucked in the arc of his filiated wing,

all those promises you made to God more pressing now.
(What was it you said you'd do in reparation?)

God's wrath, it warns, is coming, is already come.
You need only look about you.

God gives no quarter—will never give—
to the fallen Morning Star.

Song of a Lunatic Prelate

—after John Berryman

You need not hear the footfall of my boot
upon the stair to know that I am coming.

I need not touch you for you to feel the cure,
my laying on of hands, the whisper of contact,

your dusk-red areolae swelling in response.
You need not hear my voice for spring

to arrive. Rain nipples the lake.
March winds etherize the mounds

of that frozen knell that calls you.
What of the Franciscan who sends you home

with a flog and recommends you take the veil?
You have flailed the anchorage of your body

long enough. A sacerdotal red licks
your loins. The suppurating

of pine resin pops and whistles in flame,
and if you told what you saw in fire,

no one would believe your tales.
Crisomated, ordained, by the name

you give yourself at night—
Vixen Adorer of the Bloodied Face,

Magenta Effigy of the Sacred Wound—
do you think that it is any other than He

who speaks to you now? Do my bidding—
akimbo, supine. The bread must be only bread,

and flesh be flesh,
before a god can put its gladness on.

Patriarchy

When asked how she reached the pinnacle,
a great woman scholar replied: *Patriarchy.*

Every woman rides its back as on a palanquin.
Life is an iceberg, and I am at its tip.

For every woman above the waterline,
there are seven who ride the chiseled slide

into the frigid waters below. We heard
the icy cries of those who had lost their perch.

My mother was not afraid. *Better an eel,*
my mother said, *than a bird living in a gilded cage.*

Indeed, my father's providence kept us from the mere.
Some said that he'd have been happier

had he married a more docile woman,
but docile women were not my father's match.

For my mother, patriarchy was not an altogether
satisfactory arrangement—her dry comment

from beyond the grave.

The Eel

In October,
when the clocks turn back,

there begins the cool retreat.
Can you feel me falling,

ghosting through you
when day divides in two?

Who expects to find me in ordinary waters,
summering in ooze?

Why do you fishwives need to nail me to a plank
and strip me like an opera glove?

Why do you need to smother me in sauce?
Have you forgotten the body's fuse?

Do I remind you of what's hauled up from depths,
of what you wish to never see?

Is my writhing too explicit,
the shiver of a bone exposed?

In the foghorns that call lost ships,
in the song of the blue-eyed dog that croons,

do you hear what, in yourselves, is lost,
is not sufficiently alive?

Do you taste yourself too much,
the taint of some pain

come from far away—
the unstrung pearl, the body tolling its mournful bell?

In the insomniac hour,
a little of me remains.

Can you smell me on your hands?
Can you feel my eyes that never shut?

The gods are dead,
the rivers fished dry.

When you taste my smoke,
do you feel the vigor of my buck

against the iron pail,
sisters of this one you want hunted to extinction?

Auguste

I showed her where to find the gold,
  but the gold she finds is truly hers.
  —Auguste Rodin

You are neither the gold nor the mine nor the muse
nor the persimmon pulp used as bootblack to weatherproof

my soles from the muck of the rue de Varenne.
You are not even the ticket taker

at the Lard Museum.
Your hands have cracked the bone, severed

the cord, scooped the brains from the fatted
calf. Lover of intensity, intense lover,

your affairs have sent me down
this cul-de-sac more times than I can name,

the others always other than they really are.
What better hands than yours to take the gun

away from me, to wipe the blood from my hands,
to put the severed tongue back in my head,

you who know every part of my body and have found
a use for it. Lathed in the sauce of truth,

my boiled tongue, what would it say, if it could talk?
Who better to sculpt *The Gates of Hell*?

I am wild like the nettle and dangerous
behind the gate. I who feel the world spin

when others think it still, what part of me
will you serve up tonight: broth of dog in manger,

ministra of mixed motives, breasts oozing their *volupté?*
In the asylum, love's menu is always made in the mind.

Dean of Instruction

To please the good ol' boys,
you unwrap the fine cigars,

Dominicans with their cummerbunds and golden cursives,
the sugared cures wafting from the humidor,

no Swisher Sweets, no Perfectos—
coffin nails, fags, snuff, dog turds, stogies, skag—

the language of a man's tobacco.
To perform this rite, you purchase cedar boxes

painted in the pastel colors of new republics
that remind you of the Bay of Pigs,

Khrushchev and his shoe, missiles pointed in your direction.
Women trussed in red bodices beckon:

Sink your anchor here, boys. Bloom where you're planted:
A stogie's for a man who loves to plant a hard crop

in hard soil. Fresh from the Mass and the three-hour fast,
your sloe-eyed sisters with their unreflecting eyes

and chapel veils want their priest to be a man and their men
worth worshipping. They say it would seem unnatural

any other way. You suck the whiskey syrup from the bottom
of the julep glass. You don't argue. You're the dean of instruction

in a small town where everyone is jumping off the bridge
or pouring Lysol on Wonder Bread. Another victim, sixteen and ignorant,

stares from her cameo in the paper, her neck crushed under the wheel
of her boyfriend's truck, the red soil jammed up her crease, the tire treads

across her breasts where some say a woman's soul is.
You always slit the throat of the rarest fawn, just because you can.

The deer would come to the edge of a stand of sycamores
just to watch you watch them starve,

and although they were out of season, you shot.
Seventeen jumped off the bridge this year, thrown off.

The chassis of Antonio Padilla's car
swung for weeks from the guardrails. No one pushed it

into the gorge. Now, all the English teachers are out on strike.
You'll hire more from Dixon, dismiss the picketers as *prima donnae*

with their private rage and spell it pre-Madonna.
No one owns the language anymore. The deer are dancing, brother,

and they're on the warpath. Now that Kit Carson's genocide riders
are gone, you can see their sleek doeskins

brindle in the moonlight. Roiling back up through the sewage
upon which this town is built, sometimes you find a bone or a tuft of hair.

In this town, even those who know their way
lose themselves in the dark.

My Ántonia

Ignoring the advice of the Agricultural Survey,
my grandfather, 4 foot 6 in stocking feet,
planted a hundred acres in black walnut.

For years to come
one could see his hired man, Tiny, setting the boles,
tamping each one by hand, and my grandfather following behind him,

a gnome standing in the wake of a giant,
the trees as twisted by drought as he was.
This was his legacy:

a thousand cigar boxes covered with gypsies
and a stunted grove of black walnut.
My grandmother was the descendant of gypsies,

her dowry a whistle whittled from the tooth of a boar,
shepherd's ivory. At night, her heart-shaped planchette
spoke of arrowheads still locked in the ground

under fields of winter wheat rippling like stretched tarpaulins.
What had she brought into the house,
what kind of omen?

In the red velour book she read from,
there's a story of a Russian boy
schooled in the discipline of the harness,

of his wedding, glasses catching light like sheaths of clear bone.
Snow whorls like wheat in a granary
as the guests strike out for home,

the keening of wolves heard in the distance.
In the story, I am like Pavel.
My sledge can't outrun the fleetest of wolves.

The snow glisters under our tracks,
the pack moving like eels.
I pry the bride's fingers from steel,

unman the groom with my whip,
watch them disappear as in the wake of a ship
until none of the party is left.

I will never forget the way a tired horse founders,
a bride's blood against snow,
dawn's carillons tolling a Friday of Sorrows.

Tonight, everything ready to be harvested
climbs a black seam of ridge,
the curtains moving cauls,

the smell of cottonwood roots choking our pipes,
seeking water. My grandmother's face
turns white like a wolf's,

the muzzle's white grizzle.
There is no mistaking the animal underneath.
This was her legacy—

all this before I perfected the art of moving away.
There is nothing I would not do
to make the troika lighter.

The Caterer

I feed them
in their beautiful houses,
caviar, shavings of sweet butter,

in cathedrals of ice,
the spectacle all meant for the moment—
all of it melting—

disheveled petals discarded
onto manicured lawns.
These are to top the wedding cake.

I sculpt the dragon faces of nemesia
from hot sugar, petal by petal, by hand.
The first few hurt, but then the fingers go numb.

Did I tell you a man came to the door today
and asked for blood oranges?
I said he could pick a dozen,

but he stripped the tree bare—
blood oranges
not even ripe yet.

I kept wondering
what he would do with them
when he found they were bitter.

I have had to learn not
to go through this world
disembodied—like a pre-Raphaelite angel,

always turning to meet some ghost behind me,
some chimerical breath.
What I ache for is inhuman.

There now. The last petal's done.
And tomorrow's the wedding.
Sometimes, it seems all creation

is conspiring to give us this day.
I arrange what I like to eat on a simple plate:
slabs of bread, an inkwell of chilled butter,

slices of prosciutto marbled like placenta;
and I look out across the pool-yard
into the diamond light of the patio

and say, *Today is my wedding,*
unwitting acolyte of dazzling air.
How much harder to say:

the one who would save me
is not coming, to accept this pattern
of days without myth.

At the Amphitheatrum Flavium

From the Janus view of the Janiculum,
        a warren of restricted views.
To one's left, the Vatican. Across the river, the Jewish Ghetto
        created by an edict of a pope,
Since it is absurd and utterly inconvenient that the Jews who were . . .
        condemned by God. . . . In a face-off with the temple, the facade of
Santa Maria della Pieta invokes Isaiah's prophecy: *I have spread forth my hands*
        all day to an unbelieving people.
Inside the Amphitheatrum Flavium, we should not be
        shocked at what we find.
The oaken floorboards and even the forest from which these timbers came are gone.
        What endures endures fragmented:
the hindquarters of an ass, a woman's thimble, a torso without a head. We gather
        at the Cross.
If the image of the Crucifixion is meant to soothe, its balm is at best
        an angel holding a devil by a string.
Every era has its St. Prassede wringing her bloody sponge. When did it become
        our nature to help the tyrant to survive? No one can remember
the origin of the thing. We, the spectators register
        our complicity in empire's conquest
and demise, the individual faces no longer remembered,
        not the viscous blood-black jam
of them, the place of execution in our provenance scrubbed clean for a time.
        Our country has no reason
whatever to be ashamed, wrote Suetonius. And as a recent earthquake reminds us,
        all terra firma is lava underneath.
Here, of all the gods, it is Fortuna who presides. And now
        the lions have leapt the barrier,
and you are it, the new fresh meat of historicity. The powers want to know,
        how will you survive
this gladiator's Last Supper, this cloture of the poison tribe?

Symphony in Flesh: *The Girl in the Picture* (Phan Thi Kim Phuc)

Hungers are hard to kill when you're bereft,
the child in the viewfinder, running from the guns.
By August, there are no good mothers left.

While you burned, we slept, exhausted hedonists,
waiting for a cure. Everything worked for a time:
karaoke night at the supper club, the magic mirror ball,
but hungers are hard to kill when you're bereft.

In the South, my mother was fond of saying,
emotions are not a crime. The bourbon flowed
without regret. She endured the clans, the cleanse,
the ice cream socials, electric shock.
By August, there are no good mothers left.

I tried to help you. Everything worked for a time. I wrote
letters for a Scotch-taped girl, a lark vivisected of her music,
the scarlet experience survived by tearing off one's clothes.
Hungers are hard to kill when you're bereft.

We use *mother* here to put a name to our collective responsibility.
Mummy, mummy in the gauze, who's the fairest of them all?
Child in the burn bath, the doctors cut the infected pores,
cut layers of you away, but truth and pain wore off, and we forgot.
By August, there are no good mothers left.

Obscene voyeur, obscene victim of war,
we run down the road together, hands flailing,
eternally caught in an anterior dream.
It's hard to understand when you're anesthetized, not cured.
Hungers are hard to kill when you're bereft.
By August, there are no good mothers left.

Middle Child

You are, in a way, like the last castrato
who sang beautifully the pristine higher notes,
the one everyone silently prefers for your aplomb,
despite your brother's better looks and brilliant resume.

Now the dangerous season, Phaeton,
when you take the hearts of others
by the reins, not knowing that others
are merely mortal and made of a flesh that bleeds.

Incendiary that you are, there are
no legitimate heirs to your kingdom of flame,
only consumer and consumed,
the godhead of others' want
tongued to consummation.

Lithe and liquid in your masculinity,
you have gone from not knowing who or what
you are to knowing that you are
a player, a seducer of the universe,
on a rare and brilliant roll,
in a rare and brilliant season,
come to conquer and maraud,
your spirit called down
to try on, as if a coat, the godhead of other persons.

The voice that's pleasure is the voice that's heard.
And so to ease the birth of whom you are becoming,
you sing to all the other singers
this curiously beautiful music,
strike notes that no one else can touch.

And like Zacchaeus, we, the old ones,
our greatness gone and our lesser stature
come upon us, climb
to catch a glimpse
of your triumphal ride—
you no carpenter's son.
We hover on your voice,
never minding the mutilation.

Brush Wolf

She paces my vehicle, the coyote, outstrips it
with the joy of her striding, loping her stride,

hunger in the breakneck of morning.
I must have been her, loping,

outpacing my partner, in the swim of him,
riding astride him, in the tousle and toss.

I must have left myself on the side of the road,
somewhere behind me, in the roiling brisk

that carries, that separates one in the drift.
I left myself behind on the roadside,

my I-must-have-this for the taking,
for the care, the crosses, and sacrifice, the appetite

that was to be fed, children crying, my mother in bed,
dying, asking for caregiving, sealed with the spoils

of hoarding in love's tomb, her coyote.
I took my vehicle off-road and abandoned it,

left it as the spirit must leave the body
at death, no longer

loping, the girl unleashed,
before leashing, unbridled before, sated

after, having eaten.
The hungry will take you, whether or not.

Come out, come out, wherever you are.
Devour me, if I let you.

I am calling you, calling, to roil with me
in the here-I-come, the ready-or-not.

Symphony in Viridian and Hunter Green: *La Gioconda*

—after da Vinci

Beloved,

Have I Told You Lately That I Love You?,
the original recorded by Lulu Belle and Scotty Wiseman
in 1945, not Van Morrison, as some think.

In my mother's rendition,
you can hear the red bud and Christ's blood quicken
on the banks of the Ohio during the Passion.
How does one learn to croon like that
except through suffering?

We invent titles for your oeuvre.
The volume called *Accidental Marriage*
to be followed by its sequel *Temporary Husband.*

We, your audience, are impressed with how many times
you have chosen to remarry,
our faculty for such permanently defunct,
redirected toward the pursuit of heavenly objects,
which renders us a complete failure at this embodiment of the body
and the progeny that ensue.

Question two: Ann has become Aidan. What is the proper etiquette?
Do I refer to the first book as being written by Ann or Aidan
or do I opt for the more androgynous A.?

Question three: The sixth amendment states:
After a last serving of treacle pie,
one must not only be put to death
but understand that one is dying.
Do you understand?
Let me introduce you to the principle of erasure.

From the moment of conception, one is dying.
The more one lives, the more life itself is being erased.

If you came late to this prom,
you will have already missed the first question.
It is always a question of identity.
The subject of the *Mona Lisa* is still unknown.
The experts speculate.
Some say the Madonna, others Mary Magdalene,
still others Leonardo himself. The discovery of a second, earlier
painting suggests Leonardo's mistress.

I can no more know who you really are
than the experts know *La Gioconda*.
The real sitter now coffined in satin
molders in the ground,
a ballerina in a music box
where the figurine comes alive
upon opening the lid, then quiets
when shut.

If you visit the prison of her portrait
lacquered on Lombardy pine
you will save her,
her spirit cloistered in portraiture from time
like the subject of a moving diorama
activated by sight.

The body is a prison with a key.
When you read this, beloved,
I come alive through you
with my mother's smile.

We do not need to know her identity.
Who smiles to us from all eternity

with such knowing
but a saint?

Cloud Forest

The brugmansia's slender, fluted bells proffer their deadly champagne,
their alluring, toxic flowers dangling as if they'd been gassed—
angel's trumpet they're called—as deadly as the single carbon

bound to oxygen you inhale, motor running. An acre of trees
for each ton of carbon load is packed up these Costa Rican steeps
by human hand, the forest canopy a lung.

You are carbon after all and to dust you shall return.
You are tired of the news, each day another hemorrhagic
wound: the drilling day, the trigger point, unctuous

plumes unfurling a Medusa's head, a toxic gumbo spilling into dread.
On the path, by moonlight, just like you,
the ants are dismantling the jungle, leaf by leaf,

dragging it to their fire hill. Who would will their nature
or yours—your farm-fed fish, your terrestrian gavage—
other than it is? They've been here since the start of time,

boring holes through leaves no one read.
Genius of the lazar house, *petite âme bleue,* how long
will your species live, the earth a spinning lazaretto?

The fleshlike bells proffer their perfume.
You are of them—their syrups of forgetfulness,
their gummy shades of night. How long will it take

to remake you, your soul no longer made of lead?
Someone held the handkerchief as the world danced to its edge.
The owl asks, *Who?* You knew the answer once.

Exile

A sudden freeze, and conception fails,
a dozen snowy bracts of flame browning in the mud—
all February, the mind's haiku:

A meager beaking
through the dust for some bright bud,
hidden in decay.

Yet another ovum detaches from the womb.
The inhabitants of this place barrel on,
boil hay to mete the winter out,

a recipe for gruel torn from Calvin's book,
as if by force of will one could clear the fence
without a hitch, could keep the tiny, backyard corpse at bay.

O sparrow stunned by glass that seemed like air,
you feel half-dressed without your crown of thorns.
When was it want came insinuating, presaging

the path the heart would take, always into separation,
the bezeled jewel tumbling from its groove,
that momentary act of inattention that assigned you

to this life of convalescence? Winged, wounded,
caught between desire and the stark abstinence
of saints, you know the penance for the disobedience

that made you mortal, fallen.
Under the eaves of some ancient starlight
you wish to strip the self away, grip

some clawlike jaws—the bromeliad
with its cerise vegetation and permutations
of a fiercer life—to nullify this dullness.

Time was. You were.
Everything you touch is grist for ascension:
the soured laundry, the heart's history,

the backing of the mirror that makes
the silver luminous. In the dark
lining of your life, the ovum takes.

Survey your moment in the world,
time dangling from its lanyard.
A mere caress could break you open.

Self-Portrait as Spring

What do they call you,
your after-odor wafting through a room,

silt dredged from the lake's silk bottom,
deconstructed brew, silage,

the after-scent of your passing,
white magnolia steeped in nipple's milk,

the body made glandular again,
life odiferous:

root chakra, Earth's menses,
insouciance of red-green tridents

conjured up from winter's wearied
ground—a dog's pizzle slipping

from its sheath is the red, red rouge
of spring gliding from its case.

Be gone, decrepitude; be gone, Guantanamo.
Tonight everything is rising from the dead,

b-girls and b-boys neck beneath a street's mauve
lampière, air heavy with monsoon,

impress of a swoon a seine net cannot gather.
We are all nose in spring, and where

it leads us: to the crevices in flesh,
Eros Aprilling us into wider spaces,

intimacy of tongue on neck, all Aries root
and silk *souplesse* of Hollandaise.

How the evening greens us,
the rich, deep heart of a spade in earth, the fresh-cut

smell of chlorophyll, a vibrato moaning the dark.
It has taken this long—so long—to breathe deeply.

Paradise

All day, moths make their little stairs above the hydrangea,
trace the strings of a lyre, play the song
of beautiful skin. *Be open,* the voice says, its edges like water.
What of your shining body revealed?

You draw the blinds against the light of paradise,
against its too-generous reception, but isn't this why
you came here, to be received, to lower yourself,
not without the creaking of the windlass—

your reticence, your complaint—like a pail
into a well, finally to be immersed in another element,
in order to be filled? When was it death came flying in,
that first bolt of blue-white jay scolding from the hedge,

that voice that said to darkness, *Nothing comes of what equivocates.*
Every story is a story of the Fall. In the suburbs, one is safe.
Spring surges suddenly into June like a bad transmission,
no one in the driver's seat, the haulms of potato plants

scythed against the blight, the disease turned inward, under,
burnt. This sticky view with its evidence of an infinite
imagination at work—trees with green breasts and testicles,
the papaya's fish-egged cavity, its sequined, succulent glue—

means to turn you out, not in, to the light's inspection,
to scour you with paradise, so that the mind, surrendering
its preachments, can come down from its makeshift pulpit
to board the lighter carrying it across the water's faultless blue.

Spoilage

You've succeeded in various ways, graduated at the head
of your class (bought low, sold high, worked late),
knowing too well that the body's government will eventually fall
to its own dictates, the pristine wilderness inside
you despoiled for barrels of light
crude, already futured and making their exodus trip

south to Gambier, Ohio, where the last voters are still waiting to trip
a lever on the godhead or goat head
of the Enlightenment, a light
pollen dusting the dead. Take a number, late
bloomer. Everyone knows an inside
straight when they see one. What befalls

a legend most in Gambier is that this green-summer-gone-late-fall
gets deciduous, the whole state turning red. Take a trip.
Travel light. Tomorrow they'll be calling you spoilage. Inside
life's butcher shop, the head-
cheese maker will tell you: "There's no part of the animal that can't be used."
     Early or late,
dark meat or light, haruspex, what do you divine in these entrails? Light-

en up. *Enjoy the fall foliage.* But lately, you've begun to hear a violin wire in the light
sorrow of stairwells. What befalls a head case most is that the windfall
profits of butchery fail you, the jig and itch of apostasy up! *Don't get left outside
     this late
in life. Yes, there's St. Aignan for ringworm, Helenian for cellulitis.* He pauses
     then trips
the safety guard on the slicer. *But be prudent. Why, last week, some climbers
     scaling the head-
wall of El Cap were found frozen inside*

their harnesses. He opens the meat locker. *Want to take a look inside?*
He laughs. *Count your change before you leave, and turn out the light.*
O cathedral of shivering light, o shiv-lights of the dead! Adios, head-
tripper. Oh, things fall
into place, but don't trip
the switch on the light on your way to the head this late

at night. Alas, you learned late
what everyone else knew. You were just a dream inside
the head of a fabulist's daughter, a trip-
tych of longing for the bruised light
of October. Every figure is bruised. Every love scribes us to the deep, our pitfalls
not even our own. Swaddled in the curative light of the sanatorium, what figurehead

in white will rise late to shed light
on your Passion? Take a trip. Travel light. God is hungry. Step inside
the capsule, little towhead, and prepare for the spendthrift gorgeousness of your fall.

Crawlspace

Perhaps you came crawling to this place.
      Perhaps you forgot who you were
long ago, warden of extinguished hopes,
      keeper of the stillnesses, avatar
of what is past, your heart
      the guardian of what is obsolete.

Not monarch, not so much as moth, but pupae-hearted fool,
      this risk you had to take
for passion's sake has left the stench
      of Limbo's hearse upon you. All sins
look equal from the jailhouse of your life,
      all vistas the same.

The window's mullioned light changes nothing.
      Not he, not she, will ever deliver
you from this dust-sprent dramhouse,
      this deadly angel's veil
beneath which you can do no more
      than breathe and sleep.

Slurried by the human concourse of concern,
      fatigue has finally midwifed
you to something like compassion for the self.
      Say goodbye to this village
where the denizens have perfected
      the art of rubbing salt.

Let the sparks fly from the timbers,
      and remember that no one

is ever coming back—not you, not he,
        not the golden eagle
that used to haunt this place—to say:
        I regret.

The world has grown tired
        of your *I have just newly risen from the dead.*
Your life lies now beyond night's colander of stars.
        Become a master of change
for change is upon you.
        Deity, you have no mother but the self.

Rita

In the black lull of days after the holy days
when the Furies brew bacteria in the jellied gravies

of the bird, the silver returned to blacken in a box,
the cobwebs hanging like chandeliers, the toxic

shock of stupor set in, Rita,
what makes you chirr inside like a cicada

in another season, what makes your wings unfold?
A Maserati idling outside in a cold

alley, the silk of lovers' talk, a good bookie,
your smoky-throated slide on Scotch into half-baked

oblivion, the black-lace thong
you stow beneath your gown, the wasp-waisted epergne

of a young man's torso? He works graveyard at the home.
He'll do anything for the green—anything—and you'll pay him

with your ghost money, that money you threw away
on tournament mahjong—lust, not God, the final delectation

before your children tether you to the guardrails of a sink
to thrash like a tarred bird. You bobolink,

you always knew that there was more to be had living on the edge,
more thrills than a mortgage payment or the trimming of a hedge.

You've gerrymandered whole decades of your life with your enameled claws,
amended fangs and water wings. You married a Khan, an outlaw.

No matter the repo man, the emptied garage. Your heyday is here.
You're not afraid to walk out beyond the city limits where

the tattooed night keeps a full bar and a shack of stars.
You'll shag on a stack of last year's leaves, have sex in a car

abandoned out by the dump before you die listening to the bray
of that demented ass in 9-A.

You still want a little magic. It's the spent spells that break
you, o night waitress of the broke-and-found, out limping with your broken

dreams and worn-down heels where the macadam ends
and the dirt begins, past the fish houses and the duck blinds,

where a hunter's catcall can peel away your reticence.
Rita, don't get hysterical on me. Didn't you foresee how wet

we come into this life, how dry we exit? Not you—your breasts heavy
as overwatered oranges, full of juice, throbbing to be touched with heat.

Symphony in Titanic Gray and Red Moiré: *The End of the World*

—*after Leonor Fini*

We were so used to you in human form. Surprise us. Come into the foyer
as moted, projector light or a breath of dry ice spilling over the transom.

Kafka's Gregor has been done. His clacking mandibles take some getting used to:
fantastical antennae feeling everything, his multiplex of eyes, their fourfold vision.

Who was it said that from the edge there's a better view? Come naked,
why don't you? We will paint your portrait:

a platinum Barbie adrift in midnight waters, your dream
house torn from its moorings in storm, having drifted into a region

well beyond what might save you. How we wish that you
did not have to undergo reconstruction, earn these stripes

of spirit that will leave you dead or still alive or reincarnate
with wings—our empathy for you simply our desire not to change

projected onto the miseries of others. We pray for the gift
of your final perseverance as you walk the tightrope, not suspended high in air

but barely above ground, where, braking for phantasms, you are destined to sprout
wings or, if you occasion to stumble, learn to swim.

We simply paint, *chez nous,* the events as we see them: the subliminal hours,
the liminal shift, the carousel of human existence as it spills into Titanic waters.

We are adrift like you, *nous elus de la nuit,* more at home with the immensity
of the night, preferring dream to divine our own way out. Exit at the ledge.

We await news of your story's denouement. Will your parachute deploy?
When you pass the point of no return, report back and tell us what it looks like,

radianced with the flesh of having lived for a time on the other side. We'll send
seven swaths of lilac and the heady scent of hyacinth to revive you from the dead.

Eternity

Just once I saw Crane, swimming strongly, but never again,
a freestyle arm arcing the whitecaps,

escaped from the captivity of human form,
sure of his element.

That last glimpse so defied the gesture of suicide:
he committed his vault from the stern-side

deck of the *Orizaba* with such gusto, bidding
his indifferent audience adieu, *Goodbye, everybody,*

then disappeared over the stern railing to be parsed
in Orphean fashion, by the ship's propellers or sharks,

a young god sacrificing himself to the sun at the stroke of noon,
never to see fame wane or beauty expire,

leaving us onlookers, as the unchosen are in the Rapture,
to ponder the vicissitudes of living on.

Does he yearn for a chance to be reborn,
even as the rest of us muddle on provincially in our towns,

privy to the local gossip, a little bored but enduring to the end?
Which is worse, the wish to be given another chance to live,

even as one is living or after one is dead?
That is the divine predicament: to ransom one's life

for the prospect of finding heaven in some other, better place.
The Hasidim tell a story about the world to come.

Everything in eternity will be just as it is here:
our beds still our beds, outside the same corridor, emptying,

no heaven save what is found here, no joy not of this earth.
I have been scorched clean by black heralds,

and I will not make light of or romanticize the fire.
Death is not what the dovecote is to the dove,

not an ebb like a nib run dry of ink,
not a gold net of light tossed upon the herringbone

reticulations of wheat or a burnished halo
poised above the fescue, but the throes

of a burning I have come back from.
For Hart, I wish him the eternity of the Jews:

the Isla of Juventud, shots of dark rum at the bar,
a gratuity of horses standing in the cane.

Symphony in Yellow: *A Young Girl Reading*

—after Fragonard

When the first crocuses,
the ones called golden crowns
and the ones called midnights,

push up through February's mausoleum ground,
I think of Fragonard,
his patrons dead, the Terror over,

the stays of his golden swing now cut.
I am tempted to lie down
even though the ground is cold

and listen to the girl who speaks to us
from beyond our Februarys
when we are dying.

In the single candle of her apparition,
this meager ration
we are given to console us,

we find some calm kept as shrine.
As air is antithesis of wing,
as water is foiler of fire,

her diadem of yellow is antidote
to what affliction roughens.
Here at last, a searchlight fixed upon our nakedness,

we might repair a heart held captive by too much solitary,
might find the sclariform light by which to ascend,
rung by rung. Advance is slow since we are

slow pilgrims, distracted as we are by that feeble stream
that can charm a doubting soul—
a beguiled horde carried along by tin-canned brightness,

mincing assayers of redemption,
plagued in this season of stray imaginings, of scarce advance,
by stillborn thoughts that can't survive

outside the hospice of the mind.
Yet in her tor of sunlight, we absorb
the umbers and butters of her light—

wicks made ready by our roughening
to sop this ointment of composure.
Here, even we, the most wretched,

find fortune within her curtilage—
this life a fever in which we sweat
the virus of indifference out.

In Case of Loss, This Girl

I love the churl in *girl*, the lithe and limber span of her,
the heart half-hurled, then hurled again,

the silky clamor of each cell's perfume,
your unflayed-flower, jujube-colored love, never-ending—

intrepid, self-convicted, a torrid thing—soul-clenched
Joan of Arc, chiffon-dawn valiant of the school yard,

half horse, half human, running faster than all the rest,
our Velvet; dressed for Mass, wearing cotton gloves

and anklets, toting a pocketbook like a female banker.
What did that patent-leather purse of yours contain?

A sword, a Herkimer-diamond, rhinestone ring, a magic flame?
Was love ever more sudden or profound, lived in minnowed minutes,

resilient, green, willow-bending? Your body changed:
breasts no longer hard as unripe peaches; the eggy,

orchid buds of your fallopian tubes, once closed and private,
now open; thighs smeary with a wine-dark sea.

Angel, falcon, tyrant, fiend—where went your fleet
defense of that other girl, the dispossessed one,

who came to school waving a black banana
(o, to have a lunch and shoes!), who pressed her suit

of friendship in the cloakroom—a trinket, plastic, broken heart—
and laid it in your hands. Her name was Patty.

I miss you, fierce and valiant one, carrying your palm-sized
missalette with signature penciled in block letters

on the inside cover, as in the *Book of Life,* life God promised
you abundantly: his snow-in-June, his riot, his hunger.

In case of loss, return this girl to me.

Lüchow's

Amid the chorus of infusions, streams
of steam from copper pots, the coffee-maker
effleurages on some high note, then stems
its push of air. Then suddenly a sacred

hush descends and those who have come here
to shake cold glint of cemetery walk
stare through the windows at the dying year
and watch as flurries make their lilt and balk.

Our waiter bows then clears our table: three
quick sweeps, his trapezoid of cloth preserved
in light before he turns to leave with a step so lithe
that suddenly I think these rituals

could stave off some dying of self,
these midday havens now lost to a faster pace:
the snows of forgetfulness caught
between the lattices of escape.

Gone the wide lapels and Hamburg hats,
gone the violinist playing Richard Strauss.
Goodbye to Horn & Hardart, the automat's
glass catafalques and *gilt-edged* brew, Filene's

and Schrafft's lunchroom with its sundaes
and Christmas pudding, rumored
ghosts roaming beneath the subways,
rummaging in the bargain

basement of our loss.
All nostalgias are the same,
spun of the same Black Forest cake,
a little voodoo mixed with schmaltz

and a father's ghost. The soul,
all fire, begins to shrink
at the end of day, some flourishing away
of these bright foils against the dark

that tell us: *Time to go through what stares
back at us*—thoughts surely dank
enough to make us sink, specters of
the lives we wanted but failed to create—

to make our way as confidently as my Bronx-born
father negotiated the crowded maelstrom on 14th,
to escort his frightened daughter,
arm in arm, to his boyhood haunts.

Symphony in Ultramarine: *Columbia Jay* (Plate 96)

—*after Audubon*

As children, we listened to our father's stories
in which we were the heroes,
setting out into the forest

to meet ourselves,
our own image, our own mage.
I think this is what the dying must seek

as they begin their Cheyne-Stokes breathing,
as if climbing the mount to Assisi,
lanterns lit with oil consecrated for the Transitus,

not the wheeling of a bright city
but Plate 96 from *Birds of America,*
the garrulousness of life stilled on the page.

I think this is what I seek on the soul's journey,
through the forest, with my breadcrumbs,
to enter a thicket of something untouched and pristine,

not to be lathed with the cooked sugars of God's nougat
or to be wracked into splendor as the saint was,
but to receive something to brave the unknown.

In Audubon's plate, a perfect pair of Columbia Jays,
the male's head elegantly arced toward his partner.
What if the point of the story was this:

to find some ideal and perfect listener,
a quixotic, hermetic king in the form of a bird
perched in a *refugio* of cold starlight?

The heart is a leprosarium, said the saint.
It giveth and taketh away,
the body gone limp,

the body a mass of gold coins
the color of aspens already changing
high in the mountains.

To us, the king reveals his splendor,
poised as he is to receive us
exactly as we are.

Kairos

Be calm, said the voice;
under rubble, under refuse,
underneath everything

lies the goddess in her grotto,
handless maiden,
her limbless effigy

making things sing again
above earth:
in the boughs, almonds still gelid
in their furred casings, bee-thrum spelling

the sacral; despite damage, despite
the maiden's missing hands,
despite all that tires:
pregnancy,

sluice of the goddess's water breaking—
in every telling, the burro and peasant who find
the goddess's torso among the ruins, birth imminent.

High in the treetops
the horse chestnut's candelabra
slowly catch fire,

a little ash or residue
of ascension left between windrows,
steam of early morning dew rising.

Once again it is spring, children lifting
triangles of white bread from waxed paper
folded like the arms of the goddess,

despite everything,
until the thrum stops.

Carville Leprosarium

The squeamish need not apply.
You'd have to be half crazy

or in love to do the work. To see the light
at the hallway's end, to see God

through this palsied lens,
I had to be brought to starvation's edge

before I learned to fast.
Can you lance the pustules with a touch

that doesn't make the leper flinch? Can you bear
this ash catechism of burning

before you build again?
The disease affects the reticulated web

of nerves that filiate all extremities,
the lining of the nose.

The doctors in their white albs
speak of New Heaven and New Earth,

of research and remission, but there is no cure
for leprosy; the lesions never heal.

Are you willing to hose the cribs of blood slurry
on God's great clearing day?

Are you willing to assist in this naked, new birth?
What can't be broken down in order

to be made more useable, in order to
be used? Oh, so you thought

that you were going to cure the lepers,
that the leper wasn't you?

Then learn to sit with your despair,
seal all the doors with wax,

and listen to the death rattle of your idols
as God withdraws his face.

Carville Leprosarium. Come for the sycamores
and oaks, the manacled light.

You'd have to be half crazy
or in love to do the work. Then learn to sit

with your despair and bear
the silence of God that is.

Postscript

If you come to this starry bowl with ladle in the moonlight
and wish to strip the old self away, on a raw, clear night,

sometime go out alone, toward the end of the year
on a solitary road, limned by igneous fires, lit micas

of snow, until you reach a pasture of cattle lowing
beneath a rocky brink on a plain of continuous light;

and listen to the primordial moan
of creatures, sturdy heads hunkered,

that seek comfort and, finding none, wander.
Then if you are ready to be broken by a heaven that glisters

like granite, make a poultice of cold starlight
that siphons the heat out of being

and rarifies it, renders the soul crystalline.
Let heaven anneal your heart.

Tempered by suffering, if touched,
all that once inflamed you will shatter.

Acknowledgments

Grateful acknowledgment is made to the editors of the following publications where these poems, some of which have been subsequently revised, originally appeared:

The Antioch Review: "Dean of Instruction"

Archeopteryx: "Flame-Shirt Rag"

Chokecherries: "The Caterer"

Green Linden: "My Ántonia"

Image: A Journal of Religion and the Arts: "At the Amphitheatrum Flavium," "Molest the Dead," "Postscript," and "Symphony in Yellow: *A Young Girl Reading*"

Mandorla: "The Cutters," "Middle Child," and "Symphony in Red"

New York Encounter: "Carville Leprosarium"

Poetry East: "Cloud Forest," "Lüchow's," and "Symphony in Brimstone: *Barn Owl* (Plate 171)"

Pool: "Brush Wolf," "Epoch," "Eternity," and "Symphony in Flesh: *The Girl in the Picture* (Phan Thi Kim Phuc)"

Taos Journal of Poetry & Art: "Symphony in Ultramarine: *Columbia Jay* (Plate 96)"

Western Humanities Review: "Dementia Rag," "The Passion," "Spoilage," and "Symphony in White, No. 1: *The White Girl*"

A portion of this manuscript received the Robert H. Winner Memorial Award in 2012 from the Poetry Society of America. My thanks to Toi Derricotte for her citation.

I am greatly indebted to A. M. Fine, cofounder of Casa Libre en Solana, for the gift of refuge I received in 2007 and for his many acts of inspiration; to Veronica Golos and Andrea Watson of 3: A Taos Press, for seeing the manuscript's potential, and to Jim Schley, Jeffrey Levine, Cassandra Cleghorn, and Marie Gauthier for helping me realize it. To Mark Wunderlich, Roberto J. Tejada, and Nathan Filbert, I wish to express my thanks for their moral support along the way; to Scott Cairns, Carolyn Forché, and Jamie Ross, my abiding gratitude for their close readings of this work in manuscript; and to Richard Howard, my enduring admiration for the gift of his mentorship.

Other Books from Tupelo Press

Silver Road (hybrid memoir), Kazim Ali

A Certain Roughness in Their Syntax (poems), Jorge Aulicino,
    translated by Judith Filc

Another English: Anglophone Poems from Around the World (anthology),
    edited by Catherine Barnett and Tiphanie Yanique

Personal Science (poems), Lillian-Yvonne Bertram

Almost Human (poems), Thomas Centolella

New Cathay: Contemporary Chinese Poetry (anthology), edited by Ming Di

Rapture & the Big Bam (poems), Matt Donovan

Calazazza's Delicious Dereliction (poems), Suzanne Dracius,
    translated by Nancy Naomi Carlson

Gossip and Metaphysics: Russian Modernist Poetry and Prose (anthology),
    edited by Katie Farris, Ilya Kaminsky, and Valzhyna Mort

My Immaculate Assassin (novel), David Huddle

Darktown Follies (poems), Amaud Jamaul Johnson

Dancing in Odessa (poems), Ilya Kaminsky

A God in the House: Poets Talk About Faith (interviews),
    edited by Ilya Kaminsky and Katherine Towler

Third Voice (poems), Ruth Ellen Kocher

The Cowherd's Son (poems), Rajiv Mohabir

Marvels of the Invisible (poems), Jenny Molberg

Yes Thorn (poems), Amy Munson

Canto General: Song of the Americas (poems), Pablo Neruda,
    translated by Mariela Griffor and Jeffrey Levine

Lucky Fish (poems), Aimee Nezhukumatathil

Ex-Voto (poems), Adélia Prado, translated by Ellen Doré Watson

Why Don't We Say What We Mean? (essays), Lawrence Raab

Intimate: An American Family Photo Album (hybrid memoir), Paisley Rekdal

Thrill-Bent (novel), Jan Richman

The Voice of That Singing (poems), Juliet Rodeman

Walking Backwards (poems), Lee Sharkey

Good Bones (poems), Maggie Smith

Swallowing the Sea (essays), Lee Upton

Butch Geography (poems), Stacey Waite

See our complete list at www.tupelopress.org